What If You Just Turned Your Magic All The Way The *F*ck* On

HADIIYA BARBEL

Please visit HadiiyaBarbel.com for information regarding tour dates, bookings and speaking engagement for Hadiiya Barbel.

Cover Design by Shay Leonora Chinhengo
Photography by Keith Major and David Carlo

Published by Citadelle Publishing Llc
www.Citadellebooks.com

Consulting by Dr. Jean Alerte
www.Jeanalerte.com

ISBN: 9780692126523

HADIIYA BARBEL

"TRIBUTE TO THE TRIBE"

DEDICATION & ACKNOWLEDGMENTS

This is dedicated to my mommy who told me that I really needed to write several books, well mom here is the first one I hope I made you proud. My children who indeed are a huge part of my inspiration. By me teaching them they teach me so much about myself. To that Libra Man of mine who keeps this Free Spirited Wild Woman Sagittarius grounded and well-loved and supported.

And then comes the Tribe...

Listen up Social Media Goddess tribe, you all have given me the encouragement to continue writing and it's because of such positive feedback I've been inspired to write this guide book.

Can't forget the best consultant ever Jean Alerte, and my publisher Jickael Bazin for pushing me to get this project started and seeing it all the way through.

The team *ARAYA* who keep the core business running which has freed me up the mental space to write this guide book.

I'd like to acknowledge longtime friend and photographer, Keith Major, for such beautiful imagery and creativity on the majority of the images and cover of this book. You have always captured my essence and have consistently produced timeless images throughout the years. Makeup artist Merrell Hollis for your creativity and for beating my face with such beautiful Makeup. Stylist Ranin Karim thank you sista for your beautiful vision for my cover photo. Your style is unapologetically badass and I am grateful to have experienced your art. Thank you Oraje for creating this Crown of Locks for me and making it look so organic. Special thanks to Queen Afua and family for your spiritual nourishment and the example of perseverance as you have been a light of example, the original Goddess O.G. Baaba Heru Samaj for encouraging me to live in my truth and for supporting this Goddess work of the Divine Feminine Rising. Abraham Hicks teachings on the law of attraction has helped shift my mindset and universe immensely.

FROM THE HEART

"When Your Heart Speaks Take Good Notes"

When I write, I speak for many who are moving along in their daily life experiences. I write about the day to day internal conversations that exist in the mind. As spiritual beings having this physical experience, we find that there is always a tug of war, always a desire for balance here on Earth.

We struggle with ourselves when we aren't feeling worthy or adequate. Lots of us have to remind ourselves of who we truly are and how awesome we are just for deciding to take this journey into the physical. We are so much more than we know, so powerful beyond explanation. Our very thoughts are creating our life experiences. We are always in a place of asking and receiving whether we believe it or not.

Along the way from childhood to adulthood we were influenced by the thoughts of others, the need to please others. Our decisions based on the action of others allowing another's standards to determine our worthiness. When we begin to seek out the things that contribute to our happiness, our joy & our peace within is when we can truly discover how beautiful life really is.

On the contrary when we continue to flow through life repeating the same exact things that bring us down, that steal our light, over, and over again we are guaranteed to have a less than favorable life experience.

The great thing about being the captain of your own ship and the master of your universe is that you can always create a new experience. This is the power that connects you to your creative energy. You are the creator, the director, the mastermind, and the conductor. You can shift energy and shift the entire world around you. With practice and with focused intention you can create or recreate your reality.

INTRODUCTION

The Goddess Guide To Living Unapologetically In Her Truth.

Tribute to the Tribes: I dedicate this guide of messages to all my beautiful Goddesses. Wild woman, earth woman, career woman, married woman, single woman, young woman, millennial's, mature woman, gypsy, mermaids, sunflowers from every culture, demographics, my global goddesses, local goddesses, cultural goddesses, bawse goddesses, around the way goddesses, strippers and money flippers, and the list goes on.

We are the tribes and this, and no matter where you are from there is so much variety, yet among us there is so much separation. But there is the one thing that we can all relate to, the one thing that we are all seeking, the one thing that can change our lives forever, the one thing that will place us back on our seat of power, and that one thing is healing.

No matter who you are or where you stand in the circle of life, what link you are to the circle of life, to this chain of life, we are all thinking the same thing, inner peace, happiness, excitement, adventure, love, creativity, purpose, success, confidence, but above all these things we are seeking a deeper connection to our inner being, our true selves, our higher selves.

Throughout history we have been taught to simply accept what has been given to us, to be content with what life has given us. We have been trained to deal and just cope with the struggle. We have also been

9

taught
to stay quiet not to speak up, never to stand up for ourselves, lots of us follow behind society or behind a man, blindly. We as women have been taught to be modest to be "proper contained and controlled". We have been taught even with our sexuality to be ashamed. We have been taught

that our bodies are objects of pleasure, to be owned, to be property, to be without desire, to not have a voice or say so. Our youthful body for the gain, our bearing bodies have been shamed.

The very existence of the feminine is powerful beyond measure, so powerful that there are so many entities put in place to keep us disconnected, far away from our source of infinite power. Society constantly speaks to our consciousness, and sub-consciousness sending us subliminal messages of not being good enough. They present an unrealistic, unattainable self-image that is so easy for all of us too caught up into, as well as myself I can admit to have experienced this through media and influences of society.

We've been taught to practically hate our bodies especially through times of life transitions. Some examples are aging, the physical effects of child bearing, the ever-changing patterns of weight loss and weight gain. The purpose is control because of the fear of not being accepted by a lover, and employer, family, and society, we find ourselves chasing the next thing of desire so that we may stay in the race.

Well my goddesses I am here to tell you that you can create the game as well as play the game. You make the rules to the game and you break the rules to the game and you create and re-create the game over and over again. It is your time to shine let's rise.

What If You Just Turned Your Magic All The Way The *F*ck* On

I'm so not playing with this time that I have in the physical. I'm literally going to get exactly what I'm calling from the universe and the universal law never fails, but do we believe that we deserve it?

Straight up elevation and continuous transformation! When I reflect, I remember the challenges as if it were yesterday. I remember wondering how this was going to happen and how would I get what I needed to make the things happen. It was always about the how and the if... I had to learn to live in the present and to live my future as if it was already here. Then I began to get excited about the thought of it, eventually before I knew it I twirled myself there.

Command what you desire and **OWN IT** as if you paid for it!!! Own it and let no one take it away from you. Own it without the need to know how, when, where, and "but what if"

So yes, what if you just own the badass that you are? What if you just slay it until you make it? What if you find yourself exceeding your own limitations? What if you just keep rising, keep moving onward and upward? What if it actually will be easy?... because we humans seem to believe that everything must be a struggle in order to say we've "earned" it. Well what if I told you that you can have it by just knowing that you can. What if you just turned your magic all the way the *f*ck* on!? What if?

Mantra:

I feel the power within myself rising. I feel it so deeply and it's not surprising. I am asking and it's coming easily as the abundance is flowing freely. I am watched over. I am cared for. I am protected. The universe always gives what I ask. All is well.

Women Are On Fire When They're Happy

Don't let anything bring you down. I speak of women and happiness often. Never to exclude men from the equation, just concentrating my focus on the feminine but always feel free to receive the blessings as well men.

Yes, you are so dope when you are happy as when we are happy great things just magically happen. And magic it is the law of attraction that's always in action. When we are unhappy, we are out of alignment disconnected from who we really are. When we are happy, we attract so much more wonderful things to be happy about. For many, many, many years, it's been told that we must suffer through this lifetime and that our feelings are just feelings and they're all made up in our heads.

That thought process is so dysfunctional and our thought process is a clear indicator of how close we are to our true selves. We deserve to be happy...it is allowed...it is not some sort of gift or reward only given for a short time then ripped away from you...your happiness is your birthright, so protect it like a fortress and let nothing and no one come in between that space of you connecting with you.

Mantra:

I am happy. I receive joy. I will attract even more as I'm creating my reality. I only see the positive.

If They Caused You Pain Don't Wish Them Pain Wish Them Healing. They've Caused You Pain Because They Have Pain Inside. Hurt People Hurt People But It's Not Meant To Hurt You. They Can Only Give What They Know

Let's reason on this. Let's go deep. Hurt people hurt people. Remain who you are but have compassion even for those who have hurt you. This is how healing begins...forgiveness. Even when someone has done you wrong or accused you of doing wrong...send them love. Send them healing. Have compassion, put yourself in their shoes even if that means that you have to step down just a little bit to gain understanding. Even if that means that you have to lower your vibration to see things from their view.....although this may be difficult to do...

We must remember that we were once where they are and we are all on this life journey together. You hold your power by sending them healing.

You hold your power by sending them love

You hold your power by lifting them up.

No one person is better than the next. No one person knows more than the next. We are all simply floating through the illusion and the only thing that is real is the reality that we create.

You've Been Criticizing Yourself For Many Years And It Hasn't Gotten You Anywhere. It Hasn't Worked Right? Try Accepting Yourself As You Are And See What Happens

Listen there's way too much going on in the world as far as expectations, criticism and judgement so why do it to yourself? No one is perfect and no one was meant to be perfect but yet we continue to beat up ourselves for our flaws that naturally is simply a part of the human experience. All we can do is love and love yourself first accepting the things that can't be changed while just improving the things that can be changed. Keep growing and keep getting better that's all you can do.

Be gentle and be easy on yourself, if you are going to beat yourself up...use a feather to remind you to keep it light. Practice the acts of celebration of self. Honor your greatness and focus on all that is good, things that make you unique, and the things that make you happy.

Continue to dance to sing and to be joyful for your own life experience this is your journey your life and you are only doing the best you can. Oh and don't let anyone make you feel like you ain't shit because of your imperfections. We all got things to work on and that's inevitable. The same ones complaining about you and what do aren't doing well also got some shit they need to work on also. Don't let it get you down...just stay positive, think positive and push forward we are all in this together.

Mantra:
I am doing the best that I can. When I know better I will do better.
In this very moment I embrace all of me. I now set my spirit free.
All is well.

Trust That It Will All Work Out For Your Greater Good; Know It

Many times, when I'm writing it's because I'm feeling something in collective consciousness. The words that I write are from my soul and are also the words that I need to hear. Know that it's all working out for your greater good. Even when it just doesn't feel good. Breakdowns eventually become breakthroughs.

Things may seem like they're falling apart but more than likely their opening up. What we ask for consciously or subconsciously we will receive. Know this. When we desire change for what we are currently experiencing there's a detoxing that's taking place. Kind of like a storm of confusion....as with all storms there is a clearing. The sun must shine again...your peace must return and you will rise again. As you rise you will become stronger, wiser, more resilient than ever before.

Mantra:

It will all work out. I will be ok. Help is on the way

HADIIYA BARBEL

22

Sending Some Love To All The Girls Out There Trying To Love Themselves In A World Telling Them Not To

Yes, sending love to you, all of you. Because you are so divine just the way you are...in all your intricacies in all of your imperfections in all of your beauty in all of your variations. Remember, self-love is about owning it! It's not about particular skin color, hair texture or body type, it's about being comfortable in your own skin.

Accepting all that you are and not what society sees as the standard of beauty. This may not always be easy as the media has a way of brain washing by feeding false imagery of what loving yourself should look like...the more you don't love yourself the more they profit. Stay positive.

Mantra:

All things begin and end with me. My divine beauty comes from the divine creator of all things. I am lovely just as I am. When I choose to enhance this also makes me happy and there is beauty here.

_____

_____

_____

_____

_____

_____

_____

_____

_____

_____

_____

Magic Begins To Happen When You Redirect Your Energy To What You Desire And Not What You Do Not

It's always the dance of refocusing energy...shifting gears and creating a spiritual detour to bring yourself in alignment to what you truly want. We focus our energy so much on things that do not serve us...if we change the focus then we will attract exactly what we are wanting. What we focus on is the reality in which we manifest. The law of Attraction is ALWAYS in action.

Mantra:

I am refocusing my energy and shifting spiritually into another gear. I am powerful, productive and progressing.

_____

_____

_____

_____

_____

_____

_____

_____

_____

_____

_____

_____

You Have To Budget Your Energy Like You Would Your Pay Check

What does your energetic account look like hmmm? Because it's payday have to budget out that energy...deposit that ...hold that... ration that shit... on a budget giving it sparingly out to only deserving recipients. Become that budget planner and spend wisely.

Manage your time and manage your mind. Not everyone is deserving of your energy. Some are there just to suck you dry. Focus on who you spend your time with and where your energy is being spent. Is it bringing forth a return or are you depleted. Deposit your energy only into accounts that will bring interest and are worthy investments. Budget your time wisely.

_____

_____

_____

_____

_____

_____

_____

_____

_____

_____

_____

_____

_____

_____

Never Make Someone Else A Priority When All You Are Is An Option

It's ok to be selfish. For many generations, we were taught to be selfless. We were taught to put everything, and the needs of everyone before ourselves. As women, this is an epidemic in need of serious cure! Throughout history we are taught to suffer quietly long as everyone else is ok. The part that was missed is that everyone else is never putting you first but caring for themselves first; as they should be.

The number one rule to self-love is to put yourself first, making your well-being the top priority! Never be just an option. When you are nurturing your own personal needs first, you can offer so much more to the world as a result of being full first. From this full position, you have so much more value and therefore will become the priority to so many around you.

Leaving yourself depleted of energy, exhausted, burnt out, and without vitality will age you faster than drugs. You must always be the top priority above all, even your children, partners, family and/or work.

It's a thing called honoring Thyself and respect for one's needs. How can we expect another to honor us at the highest level when we cannot give this to ourselves?

The Comfort Zone Is A Beautiful Place, But Nothing Grows There

Discomfort … Growth often feels uncomfortable but this is the only place that change can occur. We were meant to expand, elevate, and explore new experiences...yes this is life. Keep moving, keep living and keep rising. Somehow, we trick ourselves into thinking that once we reach a certain place we will be content. We somehow believe that it's all about reaching a destination... never will there ever be a destination but what we can count on is constant transformation.

A little discomfort in necessary for you to grow. You will always get through it's just a part of the flow.

Mantra:

When I feel free there is only comfort here. I am reaching for my soul's desires. I came to this Earth to create. I am elevating beautifully

---

Being Spiritual Doesn't Mean Being A Saint

Sometimes it's not always positive and peace and love. Now give me my *f*ck*ing space so I may balance out this energy. I find myself in this mood from time to time so let me share my thoughts on this. There's always another side yes? Yes, being spiritual doesn't mean you are always positive. It means that you seek to remain as balanced as possible on this life's journey.

It's utterly impossible for any human to stay one way all the time. We are always influenced by what we are observing. The tricky thing is to choose how you want to feel, to choose how you want to flow. Things aren't always peaceful in the life of the light-seeker and energies aren't always balanced. Life happens. Some may want another to change their ways so that they may feel better. To let another's behavior determine how you feel is a forever losing battle.

I believe that when we are balanced in ourselves or at least seeking it, then all things flow with us synergistically. It all begins with our own well-being. So yes, you have the right to be spiritual and not always positive... long as you know how to find your way back home.

Mantra:

I recognize the energy that I'm feeling. I know that it's time for healing. Things come and go so this to will pass. The light is always near and this vibration will not last.

_____

_____

_____

_____

She Didn't Know She Was A Healer Until She Had No Choice But To Heal Herself

When there's no plan B, When there's no turning back...You turn within.

When healing yourself becomes life or death you choose life.

And so not only did she heal herself, she began to heal the world around her with her light she became the torch through the darkness. She was forced to sit with herself...to be with herself allowing Time and space to pass...allowing "Time and space to heal. She began to speak Love into her wounds as she learned how to sooth her soul.

She began to see her worth and she attracted those who were deserving as she put herself first.

_____

_____

_____

_____

_____

_____

_____

_____

_____

_____

_____

_____

_____

Don't Let Someone Else's Curated Life Make You Feel A Lack Of Appreciation For Your Own Reality

There's something interesting about believing that you can make things happen, to see it come forth in physical form. Social media can often get many people very confused. Some may also have a lack of appreciation for their own accomplishments, as many are lusting over another's.

Do remember that what you see online is a curated version of someone's life, or maybe even a false version. The interesting thing is that even when something may not be "real", when a person believes it long enough trust that it will manifest in the physical.

Do you realize that comparison is the number one the joy thief? Focus your energy on what feels good to you even if it hasn't happened yet. Get excited about your heart's desires and the things that set your soul on fire. The most attractive thing about a woman is not about the ratio between her waist, hips and ass, it's not about how nice she dresses or how amazing her hair is, it's not about how many designer items she flosses on the gram...although it may be quite lovely indeed...

But truly the core of all human kind is measured by how happy they are. Especially the feminine creature. When we are happy, full of joy, full of life, it is then we are fully living. True happiness cannot be curated, faked, or photoshopped. It is so real and it will give you something that you can feel... (en vogue song singing)

Mantra:

I am complete. I love everything about me. I am exactly where I need to be. I am happy and living life to the fullest.

_____

_____

_____

_____

_____

_____

_____

_____

_____

_____

_____

_____

_____

_____

_____

_____

_____

_____

_____

Shut It Down, Unplug Disconnect, Power Off!

There are times when I've just had enough! Can't answer one more call, can't do one more thing, can't look at one more text, can't write one more post, can't care for one more person, can't move one single body part. This is when I just let it go. Release all that I'm bound to, all obligations and deadlines. I remove myself from all expectations and become like stone. Unable to move, unable to smile, unable to think, unable to decide on my next move. At some point we have all experienced this. It's called shut it down, unplug, disconnect, power off!

I have learned to honor this and it has saved me from so much self-destruction. When we are not at our best how can we give our best? Women have the habit of forcing and pushing themselves as well as others beyond limitations. We believe that the more we get done the more we've accomplished no matter how much suffering we cause to ourselves and unintentionally others.

Luckily there's an alternative route. Surrender. Let's be very honest, we can never get it all done, there will never be enough time, we will always seek for some sort of perfection or self-validation. It's just so much easier to release it. In our minds the entire world is counting on us and nothing will work right if we don't show up and save the day. Know that this can only gain momentum when ignited by the mind... your pretty busy mind.

Mantra:

It is ok for me to allow myself to rest. When I am balanced and happy only then will I give my best. All is well. Everything will be just find. It's ok to take this moment for me. This is my time.

I Will No Longer Allow Negativity In My Life To Spoil All The Good Things. I Choose To Be Happy

Choose your experience, create your reality and choose happiness. It is your birthright to be happy and you deserve to feel good no matter what the world tells you. There's actually no such thing as negativity but there is such thing as higher vibrations and lower vibrations.

Negativity is also a teacher...teaching is about the things that we do not want so that we will discover what we do want. So, let's call it contrast... and through the things that we humans consider problems we are actually finding the answers in which we are seeking. All things are necessary for our expansion and for us to continue to move and flow through our life experiences. All things both what we consider good or bad are actually just equal sides of the sun.

Mantra:

The contrast that I'm experiencing is just bringing me closer to my truest desires. All things will pass. Help is on its way

_____

_____

_____

_____

_____

_____

_____

_____

_____

_____

Who Ever Gives You The Most Peace Should Get Most Of Your Time

Are they bringing you peace or are they bringing you problems and this goes for all of your relationships.

Yes it's important to do a roll call check to see exactly who is in your circle and what purpose are you BOTH serving one another. Your support system is the most valuable component in all relations. If you find yourself always putting out a fire, being a peacemaker, or in the middle of someone else's drama constantly....it's time to reconsider the members of your circle...but even furthermore reconsider your own level of attraction. Heal thyself first.

If your tribe is thriving and you all are progressing then you all are winning!

If you are moving through live and its nuances with a systematic flow of peace, encouragement and ultimately healing, then you and your tribe have value.

When one wins she wins for the culture. Become that Vibe to attract that Tribe.

Haters Are Your Low-Key Supporters

What many call haters I call hurters. Because even your haters are your low-key supporters so show them love so we can all win. When someone is "hating on you" all they're really doing is supporting you. They want nothing more but to be a part of your forever evolving and continually evolving growth.

With their mind playing tricks on them into feeling a lack of self-worth, have compassion on them and hire them. They've watching your growth and know your business like no one else does. They've paid very close attention and deeply support your mission.

Mantra:

We are all in the together and your contribution is greatly appreciated no matter which side you choose. There's love here always.

You Are Allowed To Outgrow People

People who are too weak to follow their own dreams always find a way
to discourage yours
Now ain't that some shit!

Trust me...the people that are telling you what you should be doing and
what you shouldn't be doing are usually the people who want you to
remain on the same level as them so that their comfort won't be altered.

When you show up for yourself and go after what's yours know that you
are challenging others all around you to do the same.

Don't think that others aren't watching your every move. Some will
watch and envy or try to stop your flow, others will encourage you and
celebrate your growth.

Surround yourself with people that are likeminded moving forward and
reaching higher, onward, upward. See no limitations within thyself and

push through the obstacles and hardships along the way. There will
always be jewels to gather and the more you continue to push through
and move forward, your path then begins to open. There is your
flow...so flow with it.

Many will tell you all the things that could go wrong, or that it will take
long... but you continue to dance that dance and sing that song.

It's your life...no matter how challenging it may seem, you will always be
the Queen of your dream.

No One Warns Us Of The Amount Of Mourning That Comes With Growth

For those who are feeling heavy and need a bit of understanding this is for you. So just rest easy knowing that you are not alone. It's a part of the process... know that it will be ok... and I promise that help is on its way.

The discomfort that we experience when we are growing can make us feel like we are all alone. With expansion comes contrast. This contrast will manifest through the challenges and changes we experience that lead us out of our comfort zone.

Nothing feels normal to us anymore, relationships begin to change. Relationships will reveal to us truth whether we want to accept it or not. This truth is the basis of our heart's desires. When accompanied with pain, it is only showing us what we already knew all along. It's not always easy to let go when we are called to the next stage in life. We often want to continue on carrying the same weight into new experiences. Well my beautiful souls it is this tug of war that keeps us in mourning longer than we need to be.

When I think of suffering I think of resistance and struggle, it is the movement away from the force that's pulling you in another direction. We must work our way, little by little, into a place of allowance and surrender to the direction of the flow... and yes, we must be willing to let go.

We will eventually make it through to the other side with new perspective new energy stronger and much more resilient than ever before. We are in a constant training, a constant preparation for all things that are to come. Yes, this is life and it's never personal but you will make it through... Ease and Flow.

Mantra:

I will make my way through, with ease and flow. It's just a process of elimination. I surrender.

If You Aren't Willing To Work For It Look In The Mirror And Tell Yourself To Stop Complaining About Not Having It

That same energy spent on complaining about things that you may not have is that exact same energy needed to push you forward to where you desire to be.

That same energy spent scrolling through timelines and stalking pages of those you admire is that exact same time needed to do your OWN thing.

Be inspired yes, but be willing to do the work. Many can observe another's success and think that they're just lucky and things are just easy for them. But what I will say is that there's no successful person that will say that they didn't put in the work.

Remember that this work is not excluded to physical work, but creative thinking, being consistent, and to be willing to push your limits when the odds are against you.

Mantra

I will stop complaining

I will stop comparing

Today I will start.

Every step matters

I am worth more.

All Is Well. Even If It Isn't, I'm Going To Declare It Is. Perception Is Everything

So much going on in our day to day lives. Full of tests and challenges... also filled with many blessings and many lessons. Perception is everything. We can talk about choosing our thoughts and staying positive even when things are going buck wild... but it's not always easy nor practical.

We are powerless over others and some situations we just cannot control. There's always the one thing that can give us a sense of relief in midst of chaos and it's simply saying it's all good. Because truly it is all good, and just by shifting the thought process things have a way of turning around. No need to stress over the things that you can do nothing about.

Remember that you can choose your calm choose to simply just breathe and choose to create such a circle of protection around you that will get you through any situation... it's all in the mind. It's just life stuff... it's not even real... and it's never worth your peace of mind and it's just not that serious. Even when it seems that it is.

Forgive Yourself For Accepting Less Than What You Deserve, But Don't Do It Again

Once you realize that you are worth more, you will expect more and you'll attract more.

Therefore, you'll have no need to settle.

Keep evolving...

Keep reaching...

Keep striving...

Keep living...

It's only you against you.

_____

_____

_____

_____

_____

_____

_____

_____

_____

_____

_____

_____

_____

_____

_____

_____

Sometimes We Fall Down Because There's Something We Need To Find Down There

All things that occur in our lives have a purpose. There's always something that grabs our attention to help us grow. Yes, sometimes we fall but it was never intended for us to stay down.

Follow the way of the child. A child falls numerous amounts of times while learning how to take their first steps. This never stops the child from trying to get up again. Each time the child falls they learn how to balance themselves, their learning how to improve their skills, resilience, strength, and perseverance.

Most of all what a child can teach us is to laugh through the entire process. Eventually they begin to take steps then they may fall again before they're in consistent movement. And even when they learn to run and run fast they shall... at some point again they will fall. Such is life... Yes?

Personally, each time that I needed to elevate my life in some way there was a fall. I began to observe this experience, looking at it objectively and then saying...."Fall Down" what have you come to teach me?

Rise up and know that even in you fall down, all is well. You are great, you are evolving, becoming stronger and wiser. Your fall is just a part of the human experience.

You Are Just One Decision Away From A Totally Different Life

Just that one decision....

That one change of thought.

That one change of heart.

That one change of mind.

That one change of game and you'll life will never be the same....

Now what if you turned your magic all the way the F*ck On?

A wise woman said f*ck that shit and she never went wrong.

Now are you going to just sit back and wait, singing that same ol' song!

Or are you ready to turn that magic all the way on?!

_____

_____

_____

_____

_____

_____

_____

_____

_____

_____

_____

_____

Speak Your Truth Even If Your Voice Quivers

Speak out and speak up. Let me translate this a little bit more, speak your *f*ck*ing truth! Own every *f*ck*ing bit of exactly what you are feeling! So many times, we refuse to speak our truth just because we are concerned about how it may affect a situation or how another will receive it. We somehow convince ourselves that it will just be easier to remain quiet or silent. What we are not realizing is that we are quietly dying inside when we hide our truth.

We are robbing ourselves of our birthright, our voice matters in even the day to day situations. Our truth matters in all relationships both business and personal. Never quiet your feelings and hush them away because of the fear of disappointing another. Yes, walk with love in all things but don't get walked on. There's no such thing as intimidation, it only exists when you are creating it... in your own mind. Although the efforts of this may present itself to you, you do not have to comply. When you don't speak your truth it's only causing YOU to suffer. Be fearless my people even if it means letting go, you are free. My writing is therapy for me and so many others... live freely in your truth.

_____
_____
_____
_____
_____
_____
_____
_____
_____
_____
_____
_____
_____
_____
_____
_____
_____
_____
_____
_____
_____
_____
_____

Big Shout-Out To The Females Not Afraid To Complement Each Other Because That Jealousy Shit Is Dead

Yes, it's so played out. I love me some beautiful women! I must have them all around me at all times. That's why I enhance them then marvel at the creation. Yes, we are beautiful. No need to envy or to be jealous of one another... you just focus on being the best you for you and compliment those you admire... it just feels better for all involved. Jealousy was a thing of the past, at least I hope to believe.

It's such an important subject to discuss as the feeling of envy and jealousy can show its ugly head in many ways. If you are someone prone to getting bitten by the ugly green monster just know that it's not a part of your natural flow. Society teaches us to compete and compare and to move so far away from our beauty already there. If you envy them just compliment them, it will release negativity from within you so that you may find they're no different than you.

Mantra:

I am unique and there's a beauty that is me which is of great value. Just as I see the beauty in others I can also see it within myself. We are nature, coming from nature, surrounded by the beauty of nature and nothing is lacking.

Some Will Only Love You As Long As You Are Able To Fit In Their Box. Don't Be Afraid To Disappoint

I'm disappointing them left, right, up and down and sideways... all day every day and night. For open-minds only and if you feel the need to control another's life flow... or be controlled by fear. Let me break it down to help you in your process, this one is for you to free yourself. Break free from your mental chains, live in your truth. I always find it so interesting when people want to project their beliefs on another. They want to tell you how you should be, how you should carry yourself, how you should dress, and tell you what's YOUR belief.

What you do is what you do and what I do is what I do...this is the fabric that makes life full of variety and interest. When someone is projecting their religious beliefs or spiritual beliefs or social beliefs of conduct... their belief of projected appearance... (the list goes on) it's because they've been taught only how to exist in a way where they must be controlled. Most of these types then want to control another's life process, robbing them of their freedom of choice and the ability to have their own voice.

They use fear to control as this is all that they've known. The other side to this is that most of those wanting to put you in a box are the same exact ones who deeply desire to be free from their own captivity. Recognize them when you encounter them... remain strong in your own truth... this is your life to live and you have every right to be who you really came here to be. Don't let society, negative people full of their own sorrow due to their own lack of self-love, steal your peace. Free yourself from your conformity, you will begin to truly live when you release.

Perks Of Being An Adult, No One Tells You What To Do. Downs Of Being An Adult, No One Tells You What To Do

It's all you boo and it's all on you so get your mind right to keep those coins tight. Yes, we really do feel really good once we've completed the dreaded missions of adulting. It like gives you more super powers when you actually make things happen while getting into your flow.

I don't wanna! Well we gotta do what we gotta do... Yes? So, we put in that werk so we can get in that twerk! "meditational twerk" that is someone commented on one of my dancing post and called it meditational twerks I'm like... I will use that. Just flow with it

_____

_____

_____

_____

_____

_____

_____

_____

_____

_____

_____

_____

Take Down The Layers, Remove The Veil, Make Time To Heal, It's Ok To Be Real

Fill your space with the things that make you feel alive. From the smallest to the largest. From the most-grand to the simplistic. Fill your space with all things that smell like love. All things that taste like joy. All things that feel like abundance... singing the melody of your song. Your space, your glory, you are always creating your own story.

It is this space, your sacred place, to slow down the pace, as you flow with grace.

Your space is where you may find your serenity as you return home to a calming. No more noise, no more chaos, no more shame. This is your place to release the pain.

You return to your stillness from which you've come. You have arrived back home no more work to be done. Taking down the layers, removing the veil, it's your time to heal, it's ok to be real. It's only you against you. It's only you facing you. It's only you seeing you. It's you returning to you. Listen and to your heart. Yes, feel your heart. Speak to your heart. Open your heart. Now we are ready to start....

_____
_____
_____
_____
_____
_____
_____

Stop Looking For Happiness In The Same Place Expecting A New Experience

Break the cycle and change the pattern. Try something different... change is really healthy. Most of the time we look for happiness in the same places that gave us sadness only because it's comfortable. There's a term that's often used "stick to the evil I know" or some will say "at least I know the bullshit I'm dealing with" This gives some sort of false justification of comfort in the negative.

It's this very mindset that stops many from reaching for more, reaching higher, knowing their worth, and owning every bit of it. I'm always touched when I watch so many repeat patterns expecting new experiences, expecting change from the same situation. The change that happens which allow the breakthrough is when you actually say I deserve more and really believe it.

It's an issue of self-worth, so my lovely souls, here's your mantra.

Mantra:

I am worth more. I expect more. Therefore, I am attracting more, and so I have no need to settle. All things are working out in my favor, everything is ok. Freedom is on its way.

Don't Be Afraid To Do What Everyone Else Is Not Doing

Just in case you got caught up in the smoke... blurred by the
mist, captivated by the media, afraid to take risk? This is your life, your
originality is your bliss... Making them uncomfortable when you don't fit
their list... Listen, do what brings you peace, laughter, exhilaration, and
excitement... shine bright and unapologetically

She Threw Away All Of Her Mask, And Put On Her Soul

There was no longer a need to hide. She used her soul as her guide. No longer a need to be ashamed, no longer was she to blame. She released the burden that she put upon herself. She raised her vibration and discovered her wealth. She allowed herself to forgive and then she began to live. She removed the veil. Opened her heart to feel. As she opened her eyes, she discovered that none of it was real.

Stand In Your Truth Because When You Realize That You Are Worth More, You Will Expect More And Will Attract More

The real glow up is when you stop wasting your precious time trying to become a perfect version of yourself rather than consciously enjoying who you are in this present moment.

You might as well just shine and shine bright AF!!! Because you are wasting precious time trying to find this "perfect" version of yourself to acknowledge your value. Know that you are already that person... the journey is in the present. There is no destination... only constant transformation. Nobody has figured this whole thing out, this whole life thing, like who really has figured it out? Don't get fooled by what seems like perfection in another's life. Know that we all experience to set an amount of trauma set an amount of pain for them on the struggle a certain amount of hardship. We all find our own way to make it through, we are all works in progress perfecting ourselves as we move along. There's really no right or wrong. There's really no one

who's better than you, has more than you, knows more than you, and we all reside on our own unique path, so appreciate this place in which you are in at this very moment. You will need this stepping stone to move to the next. All has value. You are valuable at every level, every step of the way.

Does What Makes You Feel Most Alive And You Will Always Thrive

We have to really remember to be mindful of the mindset of go hard, work harder, and grind.

In this society it teaches us to work many hours, with blood sweat and tears, and to just suck it up so that we will eventually win at the end. But what is success really when you are blind to the world around you?

In the western culture this is the norm but so many are dead while their living and numb to the joy of simply just living.

Missing out on the beauty of the process and the adventures of what life really has to offer. Missing out on love, family, no time for friends and I mean true friendship and even working while on vacation.

No days off, no breaks, and no life to enjoy.

This pattern can be broken and you can feel alive again. As a woman I find my peace while on my moon cycle as it allows us to cleanse and rid our bodies of what's weighing heavy in our spirit and temple while detoxing.

Life begins to look much more beautiful much more colorful and I began to become lighter and fluid.

Yes we create our life and all that we experience.

So many speak of the what if and could've and should've...it's not about having a whole bunch of money and material things either. Some living in much worse conditions in all over the world are living their best lives.

The day to day is ok but at some point we must step away to make time to play.

Don't Be Alarmed By Sudden Changes In Your Life. Things Are Not Falling Apart Or Breaking Down They Are Breaking Open. This Is Your Time

Now will you accept the invitation to walk through the door that has now been opened for you?

It's so easy to stay in a comfort zone and have no reason at all to grow

The only thing that keeps this world moving is the very change that is constant. Life is always changing, people and things are always changing... sometimes without notice.

Ah but my dear don't you worry, this is your call to action. This is your time to move and to explore the desires that you have asked for, whether you realize it or not.

Except the invitation. Welcome new beginnings. Open your mind to expand to explore and to be inspired. You have mastered where you are now, it's time to reach higher.

and so it is....

Mantra:

I embrace change

I am open to all things good

I can see great opportunities ahead

A clean and clear path is now made for me.

_____

_____

_____

_____

_____

_____

_____

_____

_____

_____

_____

_____

_____

_____

_____

_____

_____

_____

_____

_____

_____

_____

Don't Try To Change Anyone, Change How You Deal With Them

People only change when they feel it's necessary. Don't expect people to change just because it will make you more comfortable. The only thing you can change is how you react to them. Never allow someone's energy to change yours. Stay focused on you and what pleases you. Pay attention to how you feel and always make that a priority and you my love, will always win.

Hold your Power. Always hold yourself in a place of power by remaining in full control of your own actions. In this way you will never be affected by the unfavorable actions of another. Never try to change anyone as we must always remember that the change that we truly desire... that change that we truly seek can only come from our own reflection.

_____

_____

_____

_____

_____

_____

_____

_____

_____

_____

_____

You Don't Need More Time In Your Day, You Need To Decide

To decide exactly how YOU desire to spend it. To decide what's most important to you. To actually choose to live the life you want rather than follow what's already been taught.

_____

_____

_____

_____

_____

_____

_____

You Don't Need To Do It All At Once. Slow Down. Take A Breath. One Thing At A Time. And Always Remember To Spread Love To Your Heart. You Are Worth It

HADIIYA BARBEL

No need to rush or do too much at once. Be gentle...listen to your body... breathe... then do what feels good to you. As women (and men) we try to do way too much for the world around us but if we aren't balanced in ourselves first we can never be good to anyone else... remember to take some time in meditation

_____

_____

_____

_____

_____

_____

_____

_____

_____

_____

_____

_____

_____

_____

_____

_____

_____

_____

_____

72

Don't Say Maybe If You Want To Say No

Live in your own truth, do what feels good to your spirit otherwise you are only shortchanging yourself... stay true to yourself simply because it feels better to you and your inner you.

I Just Want To Publicly Declare, I Have No Idea What I'm Doing

In my younger years, I tried so very hard to prove so much to the world... to my parents... to my peers... that I was good enough and that I'd prove them wrong. I spent so much time trying to get it right... until I began to learn how powerful *we* spirit beings truly are once we discover how to allow rather than try.

_____

_____

_____

_____

_____

_____

_____

_____

_____

_____

_____

_____

_____

_____

_____

_____

_____

_____

_____

_____

_____

_____

_____

_____

_____

_____

_____

_____

People Will Only Do To You What You Allow Them To Do. The Day You Put A Stop To The Bullshit That's When You'll See They're True Colors

In case you were wondering who they truly were, so you kept giving the benefit of the doubt over and over again... trust your intuition. Put a stop to the cycle and see what comes up, it will be the truth. You better believe it.

So take control of your life by releasing them free, this also goes for those you love. When it causes more harm than good it must go.

Stop putting up with consistent bullshit from inconsistent people. This goes for family and friends also. Just because people may be ok and show up some of the time doesn't give them some sort of free pass

But one thing that is consistent and proven to be true is that when you decide to actually take control because you've had enough then all hell will break loose and then you'll see true colors. The ugliness will make its presence known but it has always been there. Many tolerate things from people because of loyalty, love, and respect thinking that things will change. They're constantly make excuses because of what "they are going through" this selfish behavior only grows and never goes away.

The more you allow it the worse it becomes. Just know that the choice is always yours. Decide on your peace of mind or others will decide to take it. Point blank.

Have no fear you deserve so much more and it's time for you to stop settling just because SOME things may be good. Your well-being comes first and the well-being for all those affected by your lack of well-being caused by YOU allowing someone else to take your power!
So yeah let them bring the storm and go through it... because when the smoke clears the power will be returned into your own hands.

Mantra:

Bring it on
I'm so here for all of it
I know that enough is enough
I am worth more and I expect more
I deserve to receive the same respect that's given.
F*ck that.
I got this.

Find A Quiet Space, You Can Call Your Own

In this space, you will connect to find your way home. We are in a world filled with so many distractions. Our attention is constantly required from energy around us. This is the human experience. Our minds are in a continuous flow of movement, so many thoughts, so many to do lists. So many demands... one too many deadlines to meet. In this cycle of "movement" how do we find rest? We often don't, so we get wound all the way up in sort of a whirlwind tornado like hurricane and we slow down when we are facing pain. Well my beautiful ones, know that you don't have to be forced into submission and the soul is always speaking but only when we quiet the mind will we hear. Set your mind free let go of your lists, find your way home. Yes, it does exist.

Find a quiet space where you can call your own. In this space, you will connect to find your way home. If you have a small room, corner of a room, bathroom, bedroom, living room, or hallway. If you have outdoor space or garden, utilize the magic of nature. Make this place in your home an alter or a moving alter. This alter is simply a place for you to clear your mind and sit still. Light your candles and play soft music. Allow the elements of your environment to resonate with you. Turn off all media/digital devices, absolutely no phone, no other energies to enter this space. Take 15 minutes or more in this space. Ideally an hour but even if less, stay consistent. This is your time to go deep, so it's not always about the quantity of time but it's the consistency that matters most.

Meditation is a practice and just as with anything else in life it gets easier the more you do it.

The simplest form is to focus on one thing. This can be music or sound waves in many forms like chimes and Tibetan bowl sounds for example. The continuous flow of the sound will begin to raise your vibration, you will begin to feel like you are no longer here. This is a good thing.

It's a beautiful thing when we can remove ourselves from a current state of reality that we've created for ourselves. We always must remind ourselves that lots of what we are experiencing we are creating therefore we have the power to recreate it over, and over again to a more desirable place of existence. Wow, we call ourselves human beings but just know that we are Spirit Beings many parts of a whole. We are divine, we are powerful.

_____

_____

_____

_____

_____

_____

_____

_____

_____

_____

_____

_____

_____

Don't Lower Your Expectations To Bring Yourself Down To Another's Vibration

You deserve so much more as you give so much more... but if you allow another to determine how you should be treated or you alter your standards to be accepted by another, then you're just a puppet on a string... constantly controlled by another's actions.

It Is Better To Be Hated For What You Are Than To Be Loved For What You Are Not

There is no need to please anyone just to be accepted. This is a false reality. I'd rather be hated for who I am and what I'm about than to be loved for living a lie. There's only one standard and that is the one that I create for myself. So many struggle with trying to please others... trying to make others happy in hopes that they will like you or accept you more

I No Longer Confuse What Is Familiar With What Feels Good

It's so easy to get it twisted. Humans just love to be comfortable so we often remain in situations. Thinking that it's easier and less effort when we know damn well it's time to move on. Yes, life must continue to move and to flow. It's really the only way we will truly grow. Familiarity can keep us complacent, stuck and stagnant.

Step out of your comfort zone and give yourself a chance to experience what it means to feel really good.

You can do it, you deserve it, it's your birthright and you are worth it.

Now own it and free yourself.

And entirely new life is waiting once you let go.

_____

_____

_____

_____

_____

_____

_____

_____

_____

_____

_____

_____

_____

_____

_____

Maybe It Won't Work Out, But Seeing If It Does Is The Best Gift You Can Ever Allow Yourself

How about maybe it will work out. Isn't life all about the thrill and the adventure and the excitement of creating over, and over again? Why deprive yourself of such pleasure? Usually the first thought when facing a new experience or challenge is maybe it won't work out, maybe I will lose, and the frightening thought of all..."what if I fail?" But if we begin to shift the thought process from negative to positive, even if we may still be nervous or afraid, we have a better chance of seeing it all the way through. What if I fly? And How wonderful it will feel when I fly so high… so freely… so effortlessly.

Begin to connect to the feeling of pleasure instead of the self-inflicted torture of worry. Go after what you want with confidence and free your mind of the false belief of failure as there's no such thing...ever. It's just life… flow through... grow through... experience and indulge in the very essence of your presence. You are here. You are valuable. And your contribution is necessary for us all as we are all together. The journey is oh so sacred.

There is so much love for you... and just because you've come to the physical, you my love are already brave... so before you ask "What if I fail?" Ask "What if I fly?" Trust that it's always working out for you, and so it is! All is well.

Mantra:

I trust the process. Life is an adventure. I've got this, just let it flow.

It's now time to fly

Choose Your Discomfort And Gain Your Comfort

Follow the flow. Growth really doesn't have to be painful if we are moving along side with the flow. Suffering comes from the desire of wanting something that you aren't allowing yourself to have. Don't be afraid to jump into the flow and move with the waves of life. Do it for the thrill of it, the joy of it, the excitement of life itself. Otherwise what's the point?

We've come to create, to plant seeds and watch them grow. Stagnation is like dying a slow death while your inner being is crying to be free. Don't be afraid, there's no such thing as failure. It's just a journey of understanding who you really are.

Energy Flows Where Energy Goes

Focus your energy on what feels good and never give your power away.

There will always be unfavorable situations coming your way from people, places, and things. Such is life and no one is exempt to it.

What you can always control is where you focus your energy. Know that when the energy flows in a certain direction it only grows and grows. There is no discrimination of negative or positive but only you can choose your direction.

For example: Someone makes a negative comment or does something just to get a reaction, you can choose to give it energy or you can simply redirect your focus.

So many people don't understand the universal law of attraction.

We are creating our own experiences by our very thoughts, and by our words. So next time something negative comes your way and you no longer want it in your movie, rewrite the script by sending it love and keep it moving.

Spending time and energy talking about it and allowing it to hold space in your mind only keeps it alive cut it off and set yourself free.

Want to keep something positive alive and want it to grow and want to have more of it? Focus on the yes in your life and the universe will respond.

_____

_____

_____

_____

All That Seems To Be Required Must Wait, Pause Realign, Take A Break

As I'm in it I'm feeling it, observing it, allowing it. But even as I'm in the storm of it I know that I will get through. Everything must stop. The world must wait. Disconnect. Unplug. Shut down. Go within. Unwind. Remember. Cut it off. Wash away. Cleanse. Reconnect. Renew. Recharge. All that is required must wait. Pause. Re-enter. Take a break. Surrender. Allow. Let go. She's always waiting... She's been calling... It's you coming home to you.

When life becomes intense and I become over-burdened and overwhelmed I remember the Cycle of the Sun and the Waves of the sea. Everything has its rhythm and all things have their flow. Some things seem that they're breaking down when actually they're breaking through. Seek the balance through the awareness that it all begins with you. So many things we cannot control and somethings simply must run their course.

The beauty of nature reminds us of the passing clouds... and so, in the process we can find relief in knowing that we will make it through. Preserve your energy as you will need the strength to make it through. Ease and Flow.

_____

_____

_____

_____

_____

_____

Your Journey Is Not The Same As Mine And My Journey Is Not The Same As Yours But We Can Meet On A Certain Path And Encourage Each Other Along The Way

Yes, let's meet somewhere along the way. Our paths may be different and the roads we take may split in different directions. What we can both agree on is that we are on a journey, a life journey seeking discovering and exploring.

We may not agree on the same walk of life but we were never meant to agree. We were never meant to be forced or controlled. We were meant to choose and explore that choice. So many want to condemn another for their choices and are wishing others to agree with their way and fit into their box. Things would flow so much easier if we'd stop trying to force our beliefs and opinions on others and just allow them to flow according to what feels good to them. We may not agree but we can still share the most powerful emotion that exist which is love. This is the core, the root, and the seed to acceptance of self.

A Wise Woman Says "Fuck This Shit" And Lives Happily Ever After In The End

As funny as this may seem there is true power in "fuck that shit"! Do you know how many women have gained control over their lives and put their future into their own hands by saying "*f*ck* that shit"?

"Fuck that shit" means I will no longer tolerate the bullshit... "Fuck that shit" means I am ready to take control of my life independently.

"Fuck that shit" means that I will no longer make excuses.

"Fuck that shit" means I deserve to be happy and not be swimming in my own sadness.

"Fuck that shit" means I'm going to win I'm in it for the win.

"Fuck that shit" means nothing will stop me I will be on fuck with the bull unstoppable and fucking unbothered. "Fuck that shit" means that I am returning to my wild woman ways, in my most wild woman form, living freely happily unapologetically.

"Fuck that shit" means fuck that shit is over, it's done and my new life has begun.

Mantra:

Now say it with me "Fuck that shit!"

_____

_____

_____

_____

_____

_____

Stop Trying To Create A New You Around The Same Old People

Sometimes you have to step away from your current circle and be open to new experiences. Growth comes with change and change with growth. It's ok to vibe with a new tribe that can encourage your rise!

Surround yourself with the winning circle who also wants to see you win with them.

It's always best to be amongst the people that are in the direction of which you desire to go.

When you are starting a new life, you have to be willing to leave some of the old life behind.

This includes old behaviors and old patterns as well. As you are transforming into which you would like to be you will notice that you no longer have a desire for the old ways. Therefore, you no longer fit in to what was normally comfortable for you. You will no longer be excepted, you will be asked to go back to the old you. Be aware of what you take in. The things that you listen to in the circle that you keep. All these things have effect on you and they eventually become you. The same thing goes for the New you. Involve yourself in the activities of which you like, see yourself there. Find out what kind of things do positive people do, what do they read? What keep them grounded?

Focused and on the path of constant transformation and discovery.

Don't Mess Around With The Energy That You Let Into Your Life Choose Places Partners In Conversations Wisely They Become You

Choose wisely as it's all energy and even though you may not see it, trust that you'll always feel it. It will always affect you in some way or another. Some energies are not so easy to let go, so be cautious as not everyone should take a seat at the table, not everything should be allowed through the gates, and not every conversation is worth your time and energy

Be careful about the company you keep and places you attend. Be mindful of even the pages that you follow or the gossip that you hear.

All is energy, and energy has a flow of its own. It moves freely, it doesn't discriminate. Choose wisely!

_____

_____

_____

_____

_____

_____

_____

_____

_____

_____

_____

You Know You Have Mastered A Soul Lesson When The Situation Has Not Changed But The Way You Respond Has. This Is True Energy Of Self-Mastery

Otherwise it will just show up in many different forms until you have tapped into the mastery and graduated from one level to the next. I often find myself in reflective mode whenever I'm faced with a challenge. I resist the temptation that comes with blaming others and always turn that energy back around to myself. I ask this question, what part did I play in this? How can I do better? And if it is heartache and pain that has come to meet me, I ask that very heartfelt emotion this very question: What have you come to teach me?

This way when I am faced once again, and trust that we are always tested, I will respond is such a way... "oh I've been here before, I know what this feels like, I see you, and I set you free... and bless it away.

_____

_____

_____

_____

_____

_____

_____

_____

_____

_____

_____

She Remembered Who She Was And The Game Changed!

Change the game it's always in your hands. Never forget.

Never let some minor, every day bullshit, bring you down. We live in a world full of obstacles drama backstabbers and fake people.

Hurt people *hurt people* and that's just the way it is. If you slip up for a sec and bump your head real quick into forgetting your strength, just go back to where you left off... and go harder, go deeper, get stronger and rise all the way the *f*ck* up.

Turn that energy back towards who you are... the power that's really within you.

If You Are Serious About Change You Have To Go Through Uncomfortable Situations Stop Trying To Dodge It Is The Only Way You Will Grow

Now are you serious about that shit or you just passing time thinking that it will change on its own. Don't be fooled by the promise of the illusion.

Don't get caught up in people's intentions or words... what's real is what you already know and what you feel.

Pay attention, like really pay close attention. What you need to know is already written from the door. You just chose to ignore it and try to see only the positive

And, so you took that chance.

Yeah well, we all play a part in the game so there's no victims. We all have a choice and sometimes we simply are in it for the ride, the thrill, the lessons and the benefits of it all.

But when it begins to cause more harm than good, it will bring you down. Beware!!!

Ahhh yes because either way it will be uncomfortable but there's only one path of temporary discomfort that will set you free, let that shit go.

The longer we hold on and patch up holes in something that requires more than just repair, the faster we will attain what is truly desirable.

Somethings are beyond a fix or a mend... somethings just need to be let go so that you may be able to blossom. Yes, yes... must cut those weeds, snip it even when it hurts.

You know there's no turning back only time to grow

Sooo my beautiful butterflies, it's time to go through the process... even the caterpillar knew the discomfort of the cocoon would lead to the beauty of growth, a true story.

_____

_____

_____

_____

_____

_____

_____

_____

_____

_____

_____

_____

_____

_____

_____

_____

_____

_____

_____

_____

_____

Call Back Your Energy And Power And Claim It. Tomorrow Will Be A Great Day. It Begins Now

Take your power back, because joy will come in the morning. If you are reading this and are going through something that has you feeling helpless or hopeless know that it's never too late to take your power back, own it, claim it hold it and keep it because you deserve it.

Fear is an illusion just as the feeling of being powerless.

Know that all is energy and you really do have the right to feel good, really good. Protect your energy and hold your power. This is your life and you are always in control.

Believe it or not, it's in your favor to believe.

It's yours, take it back and all will be ok help is on the way rest easy, claim it, believe in yourself, you matter, you are loved, you are powerful.

_____

_____

_____

_____

_____

_____

_____

_____

_____

_____

Which Direction Would You Like To Go? We Are Creating Our Own Story Daily Whether We Decide To Participate Or Not. A Story Is Being Made…Her Story

What is your story?

Do you like the way it's flowing?

Do you want to add more or take something away?

Or would you like to recreate a new story and start all over again?

Or perhaps you may just want to start a new chapter and possibly choose new characters?

Create it with intention. Know that your input is needed and is actually required for manifestation of your soul's desire.

You are the author or your life's book.

You are also the main character choosing the characters. You decide which way you'd like to live your story. Remember that you are in control, you are more powerful than you know.

Many feel, that when they're in a situation or circumstance in life that there is no way out. Know that if there was a way in, there's always a way out. If you are in love with your life's story create more components to bring even more joy to the experience.

If you are unhappy with the story that "you've" created know that that's a very good thing, nothing has to stay the same.

You are the most valuable player, you can always change the game.

The Pussay

So yes, it's so important for us women to own every bit of who we are. Our sensuality matters. I've been speaking live about the power of the pussay and yes, I'm speaking it with an accent... Pus-Say

There's so much energy received when we are turned on into our divine feminine when we are feeling ourselves literally and figuratively. Yes, ladies you do have the right to feel yourself, love yourself and yes touch yourself, get to know yourself and fall in love with yourself over and over again.

Since the beginning of time, women were taught to be nice, to behave, to follow what they're told and taught...blindly. We were taught that our very existence was to get a man, please a man, and to learn how to keep a man... which all are fine but we were never taught to please ourselves. Now this vid may appear to be sexual and which indeed it is, as creative energy goes hand in hand with sexual energy. Both are honored and both are important as both are indeed crucial to the divine feminine

So many of us are walking this earth shut down, turned off, walking through life just getting through the day. But just think of how it would feel to free yourself and turn on the switch so that you can hear the pussay speak. She has a message for you but you must connect to her to receive. To learn more about the matters of the pussay catch me on live... usually mid-day when I catch the vibe.

_____

_____

_____

_____

_____

Our Spirit Troubles Us When We Know We Have To Make A Decision Or Do Something That Needs To Be Done

You Are not alone.

If you woke up today with heavy heart or something pulling at your spirit, there's a call waiting for your response. This is especially even more intense during retrograde so be comfortable knowing that it's not Personal... it's just change making its way.

Pain can manifest in many ways but is really not meant to hurt you. Sometimes we don't want to make a decision because we are afraid of change and what it may bring. As humans we are creatures of habit and we trick ourselves into believing that what we know is safe. What we don't see is the world of possibilities on the other side

Honestly, you can make no mistakes even though it may seem so. We all have the right to live our best lives and make magic out of this life's experience.

We cannot enter the portal of transformation without going through some sort of challenge

What hurts us more is the resistance and the fear of the unknown

But what If we just turned out magic all the way the *f*ck* on?

Can you just imagine what that would look like? What it would feel like? To remove the blockages and go forth on your journey fearlessly without anything holding you back?

Like without yourself holding you back?

It's not always easy to make life decisions and life changes but it's also not easy to be uneasy.

Social Media Has Created Jealous Behavior Over Illusions That Do Not Even Exist

Yes, we can blame it easily on social media but without social media that mindset and behavior would remain the same. What social media has done, especially Instagram, has just created a platform for the display of what's already there. There's nothing new under the sun. People have always been jealous and envious of what others have. There's always a focus on another rather than focus on self.

Many believe that some people's lives are just pure perfection without struggle, challenge, or a worry in the world.

The focus on what is on display rather than the fact that we all bleed the same color and have the same human needs.

The desire to be validated by likes and views and friends and comments is also a part of the human experience Social media did not create it, many live their lives for the approval of others.

Now in these times there's just a platform that magnifies this behavior. There's a certain amount of endorphins released when someone has told you "you've done well" this stems from the beginning... childhood.

There was always a reward for good behavior and this is where we learned validation.

And so now, we have the ability to re-train our minds and unlearn what's been taught through acceptance of self. There's really nothing wrong with celebrating another and being celebrated on any platform, but when self-esteem becomes affected and you are untrue to yourself, this is how you will find emotional, social, mental, spiritual and even physical imbalance. This is what we call social anxiety, social media life, social envy.

Socially awkward stems from trying to fit into an area that's not your lane.

Listen, you really will free yourself and live your best self when you learn how to be yourself.

There's nothing that anyone can take away from you because there's no one better than you. There's no one who's figured this life shit out. There's no one who's actually made it and now life is happily ever after. Understand that illusions are just illusions but are meant to make you believe in that person's story. It's just a story created by the author. So, when you step back and refocus your energy, you'll ask yourself, what is my story? Am I living someone else's idea of who I should be? Am I happy with my story or am I trying to imitate another's?

Do I feel the need to ask opinions of others when making decisions? Am I overly focused on what the trends are and am I trying to keep up? If you answered yes and are honest with yourself then this is the perfect time to re-evaluate who you really are. Begin to fall in love with yourself again. Know that you are of great value even in all of your intricacies and insecurities. What is insecurity anyway?

Why do most feel the need to be secure in the face of others. The security is kind of a safety which is granted once validated.

I'm here to say gtfoh and break all the rules. Time to rethink about what really matters. Remember it's only you facing you.

Mantra:

I am awesome
I have nothing to prove
My existence is valuable
I am who I am

You Can Never Please Everyone, There Will Always Be Those That Judge You. Might As Well Shine On Them... And Win Just Because You Can

"Let's all play in the playground without judging another's sand castle"
But of course this will never be the case.

We did not come to this earth to judge one another we came to this earth to explore who we really are and what we truly can be. We came to play around with our own magic that somehow, we are trying to discover. However, there's no need to discover what we already have and so we play in the playground in which we call life.

Everyone is at a different level on their path and on their journey in this life. Who are we to judge because we also were never once at the level that we may consider ourselves to be on or the elevated selves or the elevated minds that we claim that we have because with an elevated mind or a "woke" mind you would have compassion and understanding for all of the others around you. It's just so much easier for one to cast a stone or to point a finger but the root of it all is lack of self-love. When we have true love for self we have love for all humanity. Despite our beliefs or differences love is love.

_____
_____
_____
_____
_____
_____
_____
_____
_____
_____
_____
_____
_____
_____
_____
_____
_____
_____
_____
_____
_____

Attention Empaths, Givers, And Healers. You Can Water The Plants But You Can't Make It Grow. Give It What It Needs Then You Have To Let It Go

Be so protective with your energy and respect your space. Assist when you can, then release them with grace. You can never make them happy, you try your best and it's tough.

You allow your energy to be drained but it's never enough.

Insight:

Healers and Empaths are known to pour into another until there's nothing left for their personal nourishment. You may think that you are saving them but you're enabling them. Codependency is real. Don't trick yourself into thinking you're doing them a favor when healing is personal. You're are not a savior. Through my experience with working with students or even staff members I've always gotten close to them and deeply cared for their development. There's been times in my growing years especially, that I'd hire someone just because I knew them and I also needed immediate help.

This would appear to be a win-win situation but it's actually the beginning of heartache on both ends and a classic case of the savior complex with codependency. In my life experience as an entrepreneur and artist, I've always attracted interesting energies and I began to watch the pattern. It was always very similar, with similar demographics. There were those who wanted to be around because they had a need to fill. It was energy. They would be willing to go the extra mile for anything that was associated with me. What I found was that it was never about the business or its success. It was all about sucking as much energy as allowed from me as a person and in return they would give themselves beyond necessary just to gain approval.

This is a very unhealthy relationship even though it may seem like this person is "having your back" or "loyal", know that it's conditional.

Eventually they will return to what they're accustomed to, their old ways that you thought you could transform but then would be worse than when they came. It's very difficult to get a taste of the light then fall back into darkness.

To have direct access to an energy source that may not be easily duplicated. I have found that in my experience of being a giver, feeler, light worker, nurturer, healer that eventually they will always resent and parting ways will be difficult to say the least. It never ends well.

Pay attention to the cycles, the patterns, their needs and your needs. If you are finding that you are attracting the same energy sucking situation over and over, then it's time to reflect on what part you have to play in it. Learn from it, sage up, meditate it up, and move ahead with a higher respect for your energy and remember that you are always in control.

When you protect your greatest gift, your energy, your aura, you take your power back.

_____

_____

_____

_____

_____

_____

_____

_____

_____

_____

Vibes Don't Lie. Everything You Need To Know About Someone Is Written At The Door. We See What We Want To See, Yet We Doubt Ourselves And Question Our Ability To Feel. Remember As I Always Say, What You Feel Is Real. Never Second Guess

One thing that is constant is that everything repeats itself until the
lessons are learned.

When you meet someone and you are deciding on if you should move
forward in business or personal, make your decisions on that initial gut
feeling. Sometimes we want to make something work because on paper
it looks like a good fit. Logically it works, intellectually it works. But
there's a difference between intellect and intelligence. Your intellect is
all in the mind and your intelligence is all in the heart, your gut. Your
intelligence is that signal point of guidance. It gives you the warning
signs that most of us talk ourselves out of.

Many heartaches and repeated losses can be avoided when we learn to
follow the heart. We let neediness, circumstances, and overthinking
cloud our natural judgement.

I encourage you to practice listening with your root chakra listen from
your feminine parts, listen to your intelligence.

_____

_____

_____

_____

_____

_____

_____

_____

Perception Is The Game Changer

If you awoke this morning thinking of all the things that aren't going well in your life... all the things that are causing you pain or discomfort, all the things that are making you uptight upset and annoyed,

begin to shift your thought process to the things that are actually going really well... the things that make you feel really good, the memories that bring the biggest smile and laughter... and STAY THERE.

It's very difficult to shake energy when it has its hold on you. It's also very difficult to convince yourself that everything is ok when you're going through hell... trust me I get it and it never works when you're in it too deep.

But the fastest way to remove negative energy is to just redirect the mind... I call it managing your mind because that's the one thing that you can have control over. You can choose the thoughts that feel better. Even the silliest thing like thinking about the time when you ate something so delicious that made you feel like you were in heaven. This may seem meaningless but it's the smallest acts of appreciation that will turn it around just find what that thing is for you and ride that good feeling and milk it for all that it has to offer. Eventually you will have shifted your vibration to higher levels I promise you that

Anything and everything can distract your negative thought when you are in a state of gratitude and positive thought

117

Self-Love Its Nuances And Variables

Everyone has the right to decide on what self-love means to them what does it mean to you? To me self-love means not beating up on myself for making a choice that feels good to me

There is so much controversy going around in the world about a woman's personal choice and her decisions with her own body and what she decides to do with her own body.

I find this to be very contradictory and filled with contrast.

But this is life and life is full of contrast, full of choices for the variety. I think what it is, is that we want to decide what's best for everyone else because it may be best for ourselves.

We often want people to agree with us and when they do not agree with us then it appears to be that they're doing something wrong.

But when we have decided to emerge from the physical body, we've come to a place where there is no such thing as a right or wrong, the only thing that there is are choices, we have options and we own the right to choose whatever makes us feel good.

We have the right to decide, especially as women, what we want to do with our bodies whatever that is, whether it's agreed by the masses or whether it's shunned upon

The greatest gift that one can give to themselves is the gift of self-acceptance, being prepared to deal with whatever comes your way, allowing it to just roll off you, to live in a way that you are unbothered and to enjoy who you are without need for apologies.

The problem is that we are often concerned about what people may think and what people may feel and so this very thing is what robs us of our joy our Joy is our birthright.

We look at celebrity figures what popular figures mainstream figures and pop culture and entertainment and we judge them.

Naturally as humans we have tendency to be opinionated and we would like others to join our club of opinions. We just don't easily accept people as they are we don't just let them live peacefully no matter whether we agree with their choices or not.

Some of the choices of others can make some of us feel uncomfortable and we don't want to feel uncomfortable or we don't want to feel challenged and anyway we don't want to feel it all. We want things to stay as they are, we don't want to accept the alternative, we don't want to accept change.

It is the very war against others that is the exact internal reflection of the world, I'm sorry of the war within ourselves.

So, next time when you are looking at another and feeling uncomfortable with their personal choice because you may not agree with them, just look at yourself and ask yourself why are you so uncomfortable with yourself.

A Wise Woman Once Said *"Fuck That Shit"* And Lived Happily Ever After...

The End.

Made in the USA
Coppell, TX
27 October 2022